DJI AIR 3S DRONE USER GUIDE FOR BEGINNERS

Tips, Aerial Photography, Setup, and DJI Fly App Instructions Manual for New Users

By

Kara Showman

Copyright © 2024 Kara Showman,

All rights reserved

Contents

1 .... **6**
   The DJI Air 3S Drone 6
   Key Features 7
      Summary of its Specifications 8
      Safety Precautions 11

2. .... **14**
   Getting Started with DJI Air 3S 14
      First Impressions 14
   Installing the Propellers 16
   How to Set Up the Remote Controller 19

3. .... **22**
   First-Time Setup 22
      Powering On the DJI Air 3S 22
   How to Connect the Drone to the DJI Fly App 24
   Activating the DJI Air 3S Drone 26
   Firmware Updates 28
   Calibrating the Drone 30

4 .... **32**
   Pre-Flight Checklist 32

5. .... **35**
   Basic Flight Instructions 35
      Takeoff and Landing Procedures 35

Understanding the Remote Controller 36

Using the DJI Fly App for Control 37

    Interface Walkthrough 37

    Understanding Flight Telemetry 38

6. 40

Flight Modes and Intelligent Features 40

    Normal, Sport, and Cine Modes 40

    Differences Between Modes 41

    How to Switch Modes 41

How to Use QuickShots Pre-Programmed Shots 42

    Using QuickShots: Step-by-Step 43

How to Use FocusTrack Features 44

    ActiveTrack 44

    Spotlight 44

    Point of Interest (POI) 45

Using Waypoints for Custom Flight Paths 46

7. 47

Advanced Flying Techniques 47

    Obstacle Avoidance System 47

Adjusting Flight Sensitivity and Settings 48

    Customizing Flight Controls 48

How to Fly in No-GPS Environments 50

How to Perform Advanced Maneuvers 51

- Orbiting a Subject Manually 51
- Manual Tracking 52
- Precision Landings 52
- Backwards Flying with Object Avoidance 52

8 53
- Aerial Photography and Videography 53
  - Camera, Specs and Settings 53
  - Camera Modes 53
- Adjusting ISO, Shutter Speed, and White Balance 54
- Capturing High-Quality Photos 55
  - Shooting Panoramas 55
  - Shooting Time-Lapses and hyper lapses 56
- Recording Professional-Quality Videos 57
  - Resolution and Frame Rate 58
  - Colour Profile Settings 58
- Using Gimbal Settings for Smooth Shots 59
  - Gimbal Mode Options 59
  - Adjusting Gimbal Speed 59

9 61
- Post-Flight Procedures 61
  - Safe Landing Techniques 61
  - Powering Off the Drone and Remote Controller 62
  - Reviewing and Transferring Media 62

10. 65

Drone Maintenance 65

Cleaning the Drone and Camera Lens 65

Storing the Drone and Accessories 66

Battery Maintenance and Storage Tips 66

Troubleshooting Common Issues 68

How to Handle Connection Problems 68

Solving Calibration Errors 69

11. 71

Legal Considerations and No-Fly Zones 71

Understanding Local Drone Laws and Regulations 71

FAA Registration and Certifications (for U.S. Users) 72

No-Fly Zones and How to Identify Them 73

How to Apply for Airspace Authorization 73

12. 75

Troubleshooting General Issues and Solutions 75

How to Reset the Drone 76

Contacting DJI Support 76

1

The DJI Air 3S Drone

The DJI Air 3S is designed to be a masterpiece for both amateur and professional drone enthusiasts. If you've used previous DJI models like the Air 3, you're in for a treat, as the Air 3S builds on those foundations with some significant upgrades.

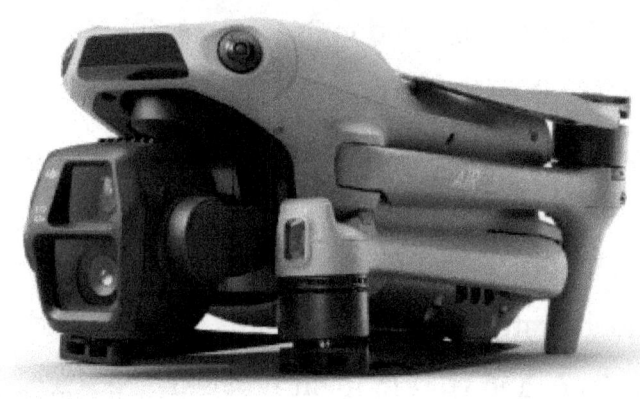

One of the most exciting features is its improved camera system. The Air 3S comes with a 1-inch sensor, which is a big leap from the Air 3's smaller 1/1.3-inch sensor. This upgrade means sharper, more vibrant photos, even in low-light conditions, making it a dream for aerial photographers looking for professional-grade quality without the need for a bulkier, high-end drone.

Design-wise, the Air 3S is slightly larger, which improves stability in windy conditions. This makes it perfect for outdoor adventures where conditions can change quickly. It also features upgraded obstacle detection, including LiDAR technology, which helps the drone avoid obstacles more effectively, ensuring safer flights even in complex environments.

Flight performance hasn't been sacrificed for these improvements either. You can expect a similar battery life to the Air 3 but with enhanced wind resistance and flight stability. Plus, DJI has introduced a new accessory, the RC Track, which can follow fast-moving objects like cars and bikes, adding an extra layer of versatility for action shots.

In short, the DJI Air 3S is a powerful, versatile drone that's sure to please both hobbyists and pros alike. It offers high-end features in a mid-range package, making it a standout in DJI's lineup.

Key Features

Designed with cutting-edge technology that will definitely excite both hobbyists and professional drone users, plus incredible features- it sports a **dual-camera system**—a 1-inch CMOS sensor for the wide-angle lens and a 1/1.3-inch sensor for the medium telephoto lens. This setup allows the Air 3S to capture stunning 50MP and 48MP images with enhanced low-light performance, making it perfect for diverse photography needs.

One of its standout features is **LiDAR technology**, which improves obstacle sensing, especially during nighttime flights or in difficult environments. For creators on the move, DJI's **RC Track** feature could be a game-changer, potentially enabling users to control the drone through a tracking beacon instead of a traditional remote.

In terms of video, the drone supports **4K video at 120fps**, allowing for slow-motion shots, and it offers **14 stops of dynamic range** for more vivid colours and contrast in your footage. You'll also appreciate the built-in **intelligent flight modes**, like QuickShots, MasterShots, and Hyperlapse, which help streamline creative shots effortlessly.

The DJI Air 3S is built with convenience in mind. It weighs just **724 grams** and has a **maximum flight time of 45 minutes**, allowing you to get more out of every flight. Its onboard storage is also expanded to **42GB**, giving more room for high-quality footage. Safety is prioritized as well, with **APAS 5.0 obstacle avoidance** and an upgraded **Return-to-Home system**.

Overall, the DJI Air 3S is set to push the boundaries of what mid-range drones can do, offering superior image quality, intelligent features, and ease of use, whether you're capturing landscapes or shooting dynamic videos on the go.

Summary of its Specifications

1. **Dual-Camera System**:

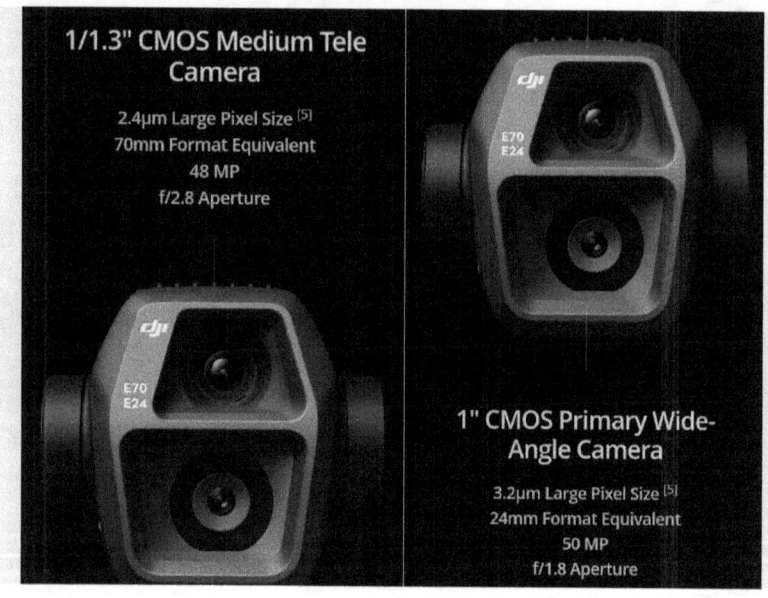

- 1-inch CMOS sensor (wide-angle)
- 1/1.3-inch sensor (medium telephoto)
- Capable of capturing **50MP and 48MP** images for stunning clarity.

2. **LiDAR Technology**:
   - Advanced obstacle sensing, especially in low-light conditions, enhances flight safety.

3. **4K Video Recording**:

- Supports **4K at 120fps**, ideal for high-quality slow-motion footage.

4. **14 Stops of Dynamic Range**:
   - It ensures more vivid colours and contrast, which is great for professional-level colour grading.

5. **DJI RC Track**:
   - A potential new feature allowing control via a tracking beacon, reducing the need for a traditional remote controller.

6. **Flight Time**:
   - **Up to 45 minutes** of flight time, giving users extended operation for longer projects.

7. **Storage**:

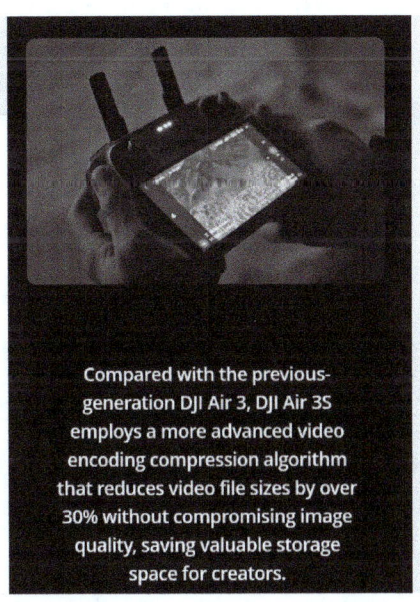

Always Ready: 42GB of Built-in Storage

DJI Air 3S comes standard with 42GB of built-in storage. This allows you to start recording right away and avoid having to deal with microSD cards.

Compared with the previous-generation DJI Air 3, DJI Air 3S employs a more advanced video encoding compression algorithm that reduces video file sizes by over 30% without compromising image quality, saving valuable storage space for creators.

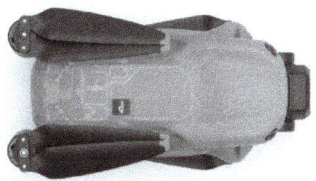

- **42GB internal storage**, providing plenty of space for onboard video recording.

8. **Intelligent Flight Modes**:
   - Features **QuickShots, MasterShots, FocusTrack, and Hyperlapse**, making creative shooting more accessible.
9. **APAS 5.0 Obstacle Avoidance**:
   - Advanced obstacle avoidance for safer flights, even in complex environments.
10. **Return-to-Home (RTH)**:
    - Enhanced system to ensure a safer return to its starting point.

Specifications:
- **Weight**: 724 grams
- **Max Flight Time**: 45 minutes
- **Camera**:
  - Wide-angle: 1-inch CMOS sensor, 50MP resolution
  - Telephoto: 1/1.3-inch sensor, 48MP resolution
- **Video Resolution**: 4K at 120fps
- **Dynamic Range**: 14 stops
- **Storage**: 42GB internal storage
- **Max Horizontal Speed**: 27 m/s

This drone is a mid-range powerhouse with professional-grade features, making it ideal for both serious hobbyists and pros.

Safety Precautions

When flying the DJI Air 3S, safety should always be a top priority to protect both the drone and its surroundings. Here are some essential safety precautions to follow:

1. Pre-Flight Check:

- **Inspect the Drone**: Before each flight, check for any damage to the propellers, battery, and body. Ensure that all components, including the camera and sensors, are working correctly.

- **Battery Check**: Always make sure the battery is fully charged before flying. Low battery levels can lead to crashes or loss of control.

2. Avoid Restricted Areas:

- **No-Fly Zones**: Always be aware of and avoid flying in restricted areas, such as near airports, military bases, or in other no-fly zones. DJI provides a geofencing feature to help keep you within safe flying zones.

- **Stay Away from Crowds**: Avoid flying over people, especially in public gatherings, as this poses a significant safety risk in case of a malfunction.

3. Keep Line of Sight:

- Always maintain visual contact with your drone. Flying beyond your line of sight increases the risk of losing control or crashing into objects.

4. Respect Weather Conditions:

- **Wind and Rain**: Avoid flying in strong winds, rain, or extreme weather. The drone may struggle to maintain stability in poor conditions, and water can damage internal components.

- **Low-Light Conditions**: Use caution when flying in low-light or nighttime environments, even with the Air 3S's LiDAR technology. Reduced visibility can affect obstacle detection and safe operation.

5. Obstacle Avoidance:

- While the DJI Air 3S has advanced obstacle sensing (APAS 5.0), it's still important to be mindful of your surroundings. Fly cautiously around obstacles like trees, buildings, or power lines.

6. Keep Safe Distances:

- Stay at least 30 meters (100 feet) away from structures and people when flying. This helps prevent accidents if the drone suddenly loses control or malfunctions.

7. Be Mindful of Altitude:

- Follow local regulations on maximum flying altitude (typically 400 feet/120 meters). This ensures the safety of other aerial vehicles and keeps you compliant with airspace rules.

8. Emergency Procedures:

- Familiarize yourself with the **Return-to-Home (RTH)** feature. In case of signal loss or low battery, this feature helps your drone return to the starting point safely.

9. Firmware and Software Updates:

- Regularly update your drone's firmware and app to ensure you have the latest features and safety enhancements. Outdated software may contain bugs or lack important safety functions.

10. Carry Insurance:

- Consider getting drone insurance, especially if you use it for professional purposes. This can cover accidental damage or liability issues.

By following these precautions, you'll help ensure a safer and more enjoyable flying experience with your DJI Air 3S.

2.

Getting Started with DJI Air 3S

First Impressions

When you first unbox the DJI Air 3S, you'll immediately notice the sleek design and sturdy build quality, typical of DJI's drones. Inside the box, you should find:

- DJI Air 3S drone
- Remote controller
- Propellers (spares included)
- Battery (and additional batteries if purchased with Fly More combo)

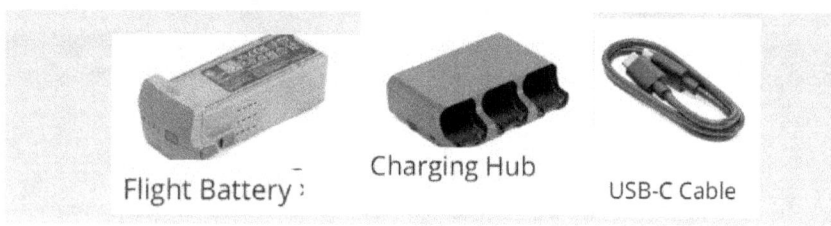

Flight Battery | Charging Hub | USB-C Cable

- Charging hub
- USB-C cables
- Instruction manual

The overall first impression is that this drone feels compact yet professional. The **dual-camera setup** stands out, along with the LiDAR sensors and a rugged finish that looks ready for outdoor use.

Charging the Batteries

Before your first flight, charging the batteries is essential to ensure a smooth experience. The DJI Air 3S comes with a smart charging hub that can charge up to three batteries consecutively, though only one battery charges at a time to optimize battery life.

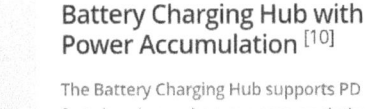

Battery Charging Hub with Power Accumulation [10]

The Battery Charging Hub supports PD fast charging and a power accumulation function, which allows you to transfer the remaining power of multiple low-power batteries into the battery with the highest remaining power. [10]

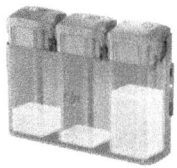

Battery Charging Process:

1. **Insert the Battery**: Place the battery into the charging hub.

2. **Connect the Charger**: Plug the charging hub into a power outlet using the included USB-C cable and power adapter.

3. **Charging Status**: The hub will indicate the charging status with LED lights. When fully charged, all the lights will remain solid.

4. **Completion**: Once the battery is fully charged, remove it and charge any additional batteries as needed.

A full charge can take around 1-2 hours, depending on the charge level of the battery when starting.

Battery Safety Tips:

1. **Charge at Room Temperature**: Avoid charging the battery in extremely hot or cold conditions. Aim for a temperature range between **10°C to 45°C** (50°F to 113°F).

2. **Use the Official Charger**: Always use the official DJI charger to avoid overloading or damaging the battery.

3. **Avoid Overcharging**: Once the battery is fully charged, disconnect it from the hub to prevent overcharging, which can reduce the battery's lifespan.

4. **Storage**: If not using the drone for an extended period, discharge the battery to about **50%** before storage to maintain its longevity.

5. **Inspect Before Use**: Always check the battery for any swelling or damage before inserting it into the drone to prevent accidents.

These steps ensure you get the most out of your DJI Air 3S's battery life while keeping your drone in safe operational condition.

Installing the Propellers

Properly installing and removing the propellers on your DJI Air 3S is crucial for safe and efficient flight. The propellers are colour-coded to ensure they are installed on the correct motors.

How to Attach the Propellers:

1. **Identify the Color-Coded Motors and Propellers**:
    - Look for the white or grey markings on both the motor and the propellers. Match the colours (white to white and grey to grey).

2. **Align the Propeller**:
    - Place the propeller on top of the motor shaft, ensuring the holes line up with the motor pegs.

3. **Press Down and Twist**:
    - Gently press the propeller down onto the motor and twist it in the direction indicated by the arrow on the

propeller until it locks in place. This should be a smooth, gentle process without excessive force.

4. **Check for Proper Installation**:
   - Ensure that the propeller is secure and not loose. If it wiggles or doesn't seem properly locked, remove and reinstall it.

How to Remove the Propellers:

1. **Hold the Motor Firmly**:
   - Hold the motor in place while you twist the propeller in the opposite direction of the installation arrow (usually counterclockwise).

2. **Lift the Propeller**:
   - Once the propeller unlocks, lift it straight off the motor shaft.

Propeller Safety Tips:

1. **Always Power Off the Drone**:
   - Before attaching or removing propellers, ensure that the drone is powered off to prevent accidental rotation.

2. **Check for Damage**:
   - Inspect the propellers regularly for cracks, chips, or warping. Damaged propellers can affect flight stability and should be replaced immediately.

3. **Install Propellers Correctly**:
   - Never force the propellers onto the motor. If they don't lock easily, check alignment. Incorrect installation can cause the drone to crash or lose control during flight.

4. **Use Only Official DJI Propellers**:

- Always use DJI-approved propellers. Third-party propellers may not meet the necessary safety and performance standards, which can lead to malfunctions.

5. **Avoid Contact with Spinning Propellers**:
    - Once the drone is powered on, never touch the propellers, as they spin rapidly and can cause injury. Keep hands and objects clear when the drone is in operation.

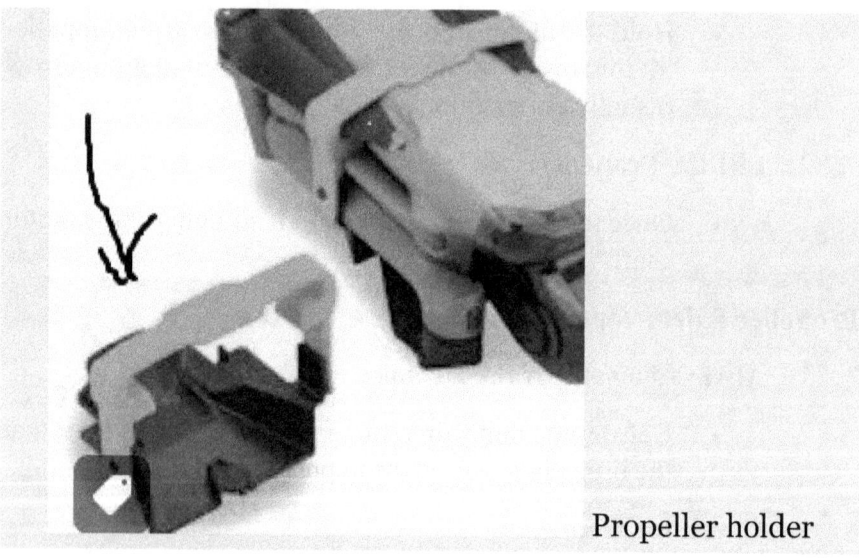

Propeller holder

These steps will help ensure that your DJI Air 3S is safely prepped for flight and that its propellers are installed correctly for optimal performance.

How to Set Up the Remote Controller

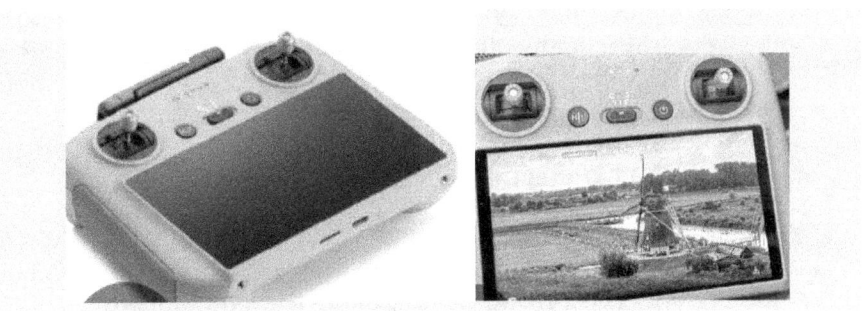

1. Connecting the Controller to the Drone

Connecting your DJI Air 3S drone to the remote controller is a quick and straightforward process. Here's how you do it:

1. **Power on the Drone**:
   - Press the power button on the drone once to check the battery status, then press and hold it until the drone powers on.

2. **Power on the Remote Controller**:
   - Press the power button on the controller the same way (press once, then press and hold to turn it on). The LED lights on the controller will light up, indicating it's powered on.

3. **Link the Controller to the Drone**:
   - Open the DJI Fly app on your mobile device and connect your phone to the controller using the provided USB cable.
   - The app will guide you through the linking process, but you can also manually pair the controller with the drone by holding down the **"link button"** on the

bottom of the drone. The drone will emit a beep to signal it's ready to pair.

- In the app, select **Link Remote Controller** and wait for the app to show the successful connection notification.

4. **Check the Connection**:

- After pairing, the live video feed from the drone's camera should appear on your mobile device through the DJI Fly app. You're now ready to take off.

2. Charging the Controller

Charging the remote controller is essential to ensure uninterrupted flight. Here's the charging process:

1. **Use the Official Charger**:

   - Connect the included USB-C charging cable to the controller's charging port.
   - Plug the other end into a power source, such as a wall adapter or a power bank. It's best to use DJI's recommended power adapters for optimal charging speed.

2. **Check Charging Indicators**:

   - The LED lights on the controller will blink while charging. When the controller is fully charged, the lights will turn solid, indicating a full charge.

3. **Charging Time**:

   - Depending on the remaining battery life, charging the controller fully may take **approximately 2-3 hours**.

Controller Safety Tips:

- **Avoid Overcharging**: Once the controller is fully charged, unplug it from the power source to avoid reducing battery health over time.
- **Use Compatible Accessories**: Always use DJI-approved cables and adapters to charge the controller, as third-party chargers may not provide the correct voltage or current.
- **Store Properly**: If you won't be using the drone for a while, make sure the controller's battery is partially charged (around 50%) before storing it. This helps maintain battery health.

These steps will have your DJI Air 3S controller ready for flight and charged up for a smooth flying experience.

3.

First-Time Setup

Powering On the DJI Air 3S

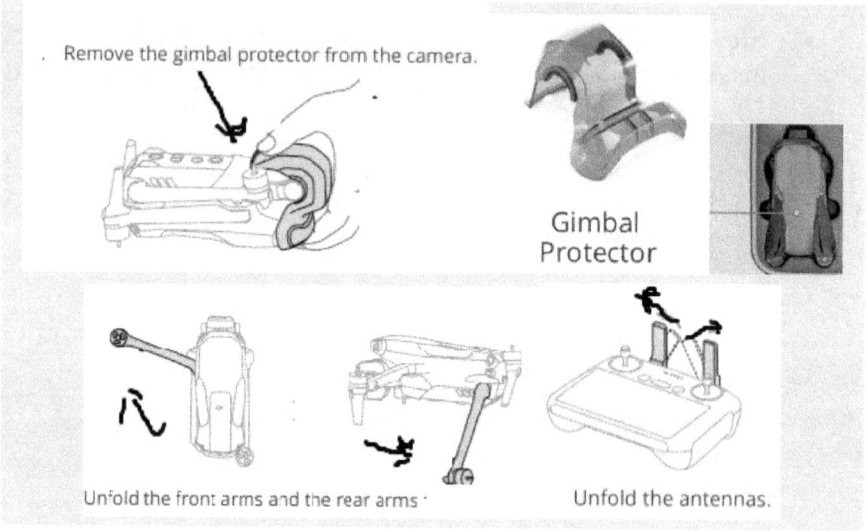

To get your DJI Air 3S ready for its first flight, follow these simple steps to power on the drone and the remote controller:

1. **Insert the Battery**:
   - Ensure the battery is fully charged, and insert it into the drone's battery compartment until it clicks into place securely.

2. **Press the Power Button on the Drone**:
   - Press the power button on the battery once to check the battery status (LED lights will show the remaining charge).

- To turn on the drone, press the power button **once**, then **press and hold** for a few seconds until the lights blink and the drone powers up.

3. **Drone Initialization**:
   - Once powered on, you'll hear a start-up sound, and the gimbal will go through its self-calibration process. The lights on the drone will blink, indicating that it's ready to connect to the remote controller.

1. **Turn on the Controller**:
   - Press the power button on the remote controller **once** to check its battery level. Then, **press and hold** the power button until the controller powers up. The LEDs will light up, showing the charge level.

2. **Connect to the Drone**:
   - The remote controller should automatically connect to the drone if both are powered on. You'll see a connection indicator on the DJI Fly app (or any other compatible DJI app you're using) when the connection is established.
   - If the controller doesn't connect automatically, refer to the previous section on **Connecting the Controller to the Drone** for manual linking instructions.

3. **Check Live Feed**:
   - Open the DJI Fly app on your mobile device, and once connected, the live video feed from the drone's camera should appear. This indicates everything is set up correctly.

Once both the drone and controller are powered on and connected, you're ready for takeoff. Make sure you're in a safe, open area for your first flight, and refer to the DJI Fly app for any additional setup guidance. Following these steps will ensure a smooth first-time setup, preparing you for a safe and enjoyable flying experience!

How to Connect the Drone to the DJI Fly App

To fully unlock the features of your DJI Air 3S, you'll need to connect it to the DJI Fly app. This app serves as the control centre, offering features like flight settings, real-time camera views, and editing tools.

1. App Installation (Android/iOS)

For Android:

- Go to the official DJI website or the Google Play Store to download the latest version of the DJI Fly app. It may not always be available on the Play Store depending on your region, so the official website is a reliable alternative.
- Download the app from the DJI website by scanning the QR code with your phone or downloading the APK file directly.

For iOS:

- Head to the Apple App Store, search for "**DJI Fly,**" and download the app.
- Once downloaded, install it on your iPhone or iPad.

2. Pairing the Drone with the DJI Fly App

Here's how to pair your DJI Air 3S with the DJI Fly app:

1. **Launch the DJI Fly App**:
    - Once installed, open the app on your smartphone or tablet.
    - Ensure that your phone is connected to the controller via the provided USB cable. The app will prompt you to enter the **DJI account login details** if this is your first time.

2. **Power on the Drone and Controller**:
   - As mentioned in the previous steps, turn on both the drone and the remote controller by pressing and holding their respective power buttons.
3. **Connect the Drone to the App**:
   - The app should automatically detect the drone once both are powered on. If not, you can manually link them by:
     - Going to the **"Connection Guide"** in the DJI Fly app.
     - Following the on-screen instructions to pair the drone with the app and the remote controller.
4. **Update Firmware**:
   - If prompted, update the firmware on both the drone and the controller to ensure you have the latest features and security patches. This may take a few minutes.
5. **Check Live View and Controls**:
   - Once connected, you'll see a live feed from the drone's camera in the app. You can now access the camera settings, and flight parameters, and start flying.

With these steps, you'll be able to fully utilize the capabilities of the DJI Fly app, from camera adjustments to advanced flight modes, making your flying experience even better.

Note:

When the aircraft is powered on but the motors are not running, the aircraft status indicators will display the current status of the aircraft.

Aircraft Status Indicators Descriptions

Normal States		
	Blinks red, yellow, and green alternately	Powering on and performing self-diagnostic tests
× 4	Blinks yellow four times	Warming up
	Blinks green slowly	GNSS enabled
× 2	Blinks green twice repeatedly	Vision systems enabled
	Blinks yellow slowly	GNSS and vision system disabled (ATTI mod enabled)
Warning States		
	Blinks yellow quickly	Remote controller signal lost
	Blinks red slowly	Takeoff is disabled (e.g., low battery) [1]
	Blinks red quickly	Critically low battery
	Solid red	Critical error
	Blinks red and yellow alternately	Compass calibration required

Activating the DJI Air 3S Drone

Before you can take off with your DJI Air 3S, you'll need to activate the drone through the DJI Fly app. This process is essential as it ensures that your drone is registered with DJI, firmware is up to date, and your warranty is activated.

Step-by-Step Activation via the DJI Fly App:

1. **Power on the Drone and Controller:**
    - As covered earlier, press and hold the power buttons on both the drone and the remote controller to turn them on.

2. **Open the DJI Fly App**:
   - Make sure your mobile device is connected to the controller via the provided USB cable, and then open the DJI Fly app.

3. **Automatic Prompt for Activation**:
   - The DJI Fly app will automatically detect the new drone and prompt you to begin the activation process. If not, select the drone from the connection menu.

4. **Login to DJI Account**:
   - If you haven't already, log in to your DJI account. If you don't have one, you'll need to create it. Your DJI account is used for drone registration, flight records, and accessing additional features.

5. **Follow On-Screen Instructions**:
   - The app will guide you through several on-screen steps. You'll be prompted to confirm that your firmware is up to date (it will check and update automatically if needed).
   - You may also be asked to agree to DJI's terms of service and privacy policy as part of the activation process.

6. **Complete Activation**:
   - After a few minutes, the activation process will be completed. The app will confirm that your DJI Air 3S is now activated and ready to fly.

Registering Your Drone with DJI:

Registering your drone is part of the activation process, but there are additional steps depending on your region:

1. **DJI Registration**:
    - The activation process through the DJI Fly app automatically registers your drone with DJI, linking it to your account. This registration also includes your warranty information and access to services like DJI Care Refresh (if purchased).
2. **FAA Registration (USA)**:
    - If you're in the United States and your drone weighs more than 0.55 lbs (250 grams), you'll also need to register your drone with the **Federal Aviation Administration (FAA)**.

Visit the FAA's drone registration website at FAADroneZone.

Register your DJI Air 3S by creating an account and paying the required registration fee (usually $5 for recreational use). Be sure to display your registration number on the drone.

If you're flying commercially, you'll need to register under **Part 107**, which involves passing the FAA's Remote Pilot Certification exam.

3. **Other Countries**:
    - Many countries have drone registration regulations. Be sure to check the requirements for your region to ensure compliance with local laws.

Once activated and registered, you can fully explore the features of your DJI Air 3S and begin flying. Make sure to keep your registration up to date to avoid any legal issues while flying.

Firmware Updates

Keeping your drone updated with the latest firmware ensures that you get access to all new features, bug fixes, and performance improvements. Here's how you can check for and update the firmware:

1. **Power on the Drone and Controller**:
   - Make sure both the drone and remote controller are powered on and connected to the DJI Fly app on your mobile device.

2. **Launch the DJI Fly App**:
   - Open the app, and it will automatically check for firmware updates once the drone and controller are connected.

3. **Check for Firmware Updates**:
   - If a new firmware version is available, a notification will pop up on the app's home screen. You can also manually check by going to:
     - **Profile > Settings > Firmware Update**.

4. **Download and Install**:
   - Tap on **Update** to begin the download process. Ensure your mobile device is connected to a stable Wi-Fi network and has enough battery life. The firmware update will be downloaded to the drone and controller.
   - Once downloaded, the app will prompt you to install the update. This process may take several minutes, and the drone will restart during the update.

After the update is complete, ensure everything is functioning correctly by testing the drone. You'll see a confirmation message once the firmware is successfully updated.

Calibrating the Drone

Drone calibration ensures that all the sensors, including the compass and Inertial Measurement Unit (IMU), are working accurately. This is important for stable flight and correct navigation.

Compass Calibration:

Compass calibration is essential to avoid navigation issues during flight. You should recalibrate the compass if you're flying in a new location or if the app notifies you of interference.

1. **Open the DJI Fly App**:
   - With the drone powered on and connected, navigate to the **Safety** settings in the app.

2. **Initiate Compass Calibration**:
   - Under the **Sensors** section, tap on **Compass Calibration**.
   - The app will guide you through the process.

3. **Follow On-Screen Instructions**:
   - You'll be asked to pick up the drone and rotate it horizontally (360 degrees) until the app prompts you to rotate it vertically.
   - Rotate the drone with the camera facing downward until the calibration is complete.

4. **Complete the Calibration**:
   - Once done, the app will notify you that the compass is calibrated and ready for flight. Avoid metal objects or electronic interference when performing this calibration.

IMU Calibration:

The IMU (Inertial Measurement Unit) is responsible for keeping the drone stable by detecting motion, rotation, and acceleration. Calibration is needed if the drone behaves erratically during flight or if prompted by the app.

1. **Go to IMU Calibration**:
    - In the DJI Fly app, navigate to **Safety > Sensors**, and tap **Calibrate IMU**.

2. **Place the Drone on a Flat Surface**:
    - Set the drone on a level surface away from magnetic interference and objects that could disturb the calibration.

3. **Follow the Instructions**:
    - The app will prompt you to position the drone in various orientations (front, back, left, right, etc.). Follow each step carefully as the drone goes through its calibration phases.

4. **Wait for Completion**:
    - Once finished, the app will confirm that the IMU calibration is complete. You're now ready for flight.

4.

Pre-Flight Checklist

Before you launch your DJI Air 3S drone, it's vital to perform a pre-flight checklist to ensure safety and optimal performance. Here are the key checks to make:

1. Checking Battery Levels

- **Drone Battery**:
    - Ensure the drone's battery is fully charged. Check the battery level through the DJI Fly app or by pressing the battery button to see the LED indicators.
    - If the battery level is low, recharge it before flying. DJI recommends flying with at least **20% battery** remaining for a safe return.
- **Remote Controller Battery**:
    - Don't forget to check the remote controller's battery level as well. Ensure it's adequately charged for your flying session.

2. Assessing Weather Conditions

- **Wind Speed**:
    - Check local wind conditions. The DJI Air 3S can handle winds up to around **20-25 mph**, but flying in higher winds can affect stability and control.
- **Precipitation and Temperature**:
    - Avoid flying in rain or snow. Also, consider the temperature; the drone operates best between **32°F and 104°F (0°C and 40°C)**. Extremely low or high

temperatures can impact battery performance and flight time.

- **Visibility**:
    - Ensure good visibility. If it's foggy, overcast, or dark, it's best to postpone your flight.

3. Ensuring GPS Connection

- **Check GPS Signal**:
    - Before taking off, confirm that the drone has a strong GPS signal. This is essential for features like **GPS positioning** and **return-to-home (RTH)** functionality.
    - Wait for at least **7-10 satellites** to connect for optimal accuracy. You can check the GPS status in the DJI Fly app.
- **Home Point Setting**:
    - Make sure the home point is set correctly in the app before takeoff. This will ensure your drone knows where to return in case of an emergency.

4. Inspecting the Drone for Any Damage

- **Physical Inspection**:
    - Conduct a thorough visual inspection of the drone. Look for any visible signs of damage, such as cracks, loose components, or any dirt that might affect flight performance.
- **Propellers**:
    - Check the propellers for nicks, bends, or cracks. Ensure they are securely attached and free from any debris.

- **Camera and Gimbal**:
    - Ensure the camera and gimbal are clean and functioning correctly. Remove any protective covers before the flight.

This pre-flight checklist can enhance safety and ensure a smooth flying experience with your DJI Air 3S. Always remember that a little preparation goes a long way in preventing issues during your flight.

5.

Basic Flight Instructions

Flying the DJI Air 3S is a rewarding experience, and understanding the basic flight instructions is also good for smooth operation. Here's a guide on powering the drone on and off, takeoff and landing procedures, and a rundown of the remote controller functions.

- **Powering On**:
    1. **Insert the Battery**: Make sure the battery is securely inserted into the drone.
    2. **Press the Power Button**: Press the power button on the battery once to check the status, then press and hold it until the drone powers up. You'll hear a sound and see the lights illuminate.

- **Powering Off**:
    1. **Press and Hold the Power Button**: To turn off the drone, press and hold the power button until the lights turn off. Ensure that the drone is on a flat surface to avoid any unintentional activation of the motors.

Takeoff and Landing Procedures

- **Takeoff**:
    1. **Pre-Flight Checks**: Before takeoff, ensure that your pre-flight checklist is complete (battery levels, GPS signal, etc.).
    2. **Select Takeoff in the App**: Once you are ready, use the DJI Fly app to select the **Takeoff** option.
    3. **Manual Takeoff**: Alternatively, you can manually take off by pushing both sticks on the remote

controller downward diagonally. The drone will ascend to a safe height.

- **Landing**:

    1. **Select Landing in the App**: When you're ready to land, tap the **Landing** option in the app. The drone will automatically descend and land safely.

    2. **Manual Landing**: To land manually, slowly pull both sticks downward. Gradually lower the drone until it lands on a flat surface, then release the sticks to stop the motors.

Understanding the Remote Controller

The remote controller for the DJI Air 3S is user-friendly, with various functions and controls that allow you to pilot the drone effectively.

Joystick Functions:

- **Left Stick**:

    - **Up/Down**: Control altitude (ascend/descend).

    - **Left/Right**: Rotate the drone left or right (yaw).

- **Right Stick**:

    - **Up/Down**: Move the drone forward/backwards.

    - **Left/Right**: Move the drone left/right.

Button Guide:

- **Power Button**: Turns the remote controller on and off.

- **Return-to-Home (RTH) Button**: Initiates the return-to-home function, bringing the drone back to its takeoff point.

- **Takeoff/Landing Button**: Allows for quick takeoff or landing without using the joystick.

- **Camera Shutter Button**: Captures photos or starts/stops video recording.
- **C1 and C2 Buttons**: Customizable buttons that can be assigned to different functions in the app.

Familiarizing yourself with these basic flight instructions will help you operate with confidence. Always practice in an open area to enhance your flying skills and ensure safety.

Using the DJI Fly App for Control

The DJI Fly app is your primary tool for controlling the DJI Air 3S. It offers a user-friendly interface and comprehensive flight telemetry. Here's an overview of the app's interface and essential flight telemetry information.

Interface Walkthrough

1. **Home Screen**:
   - When you open the DJI Fly app, the home screen provides a summary of your drone's status, including battery levels, GPS signal strength, and notifications about any firmware updates.
   - At the bottom of the screen, you'll find the main controls, including **Takeoff**, **Landing**, and **Return to Home** buttons.
2. **Camera View**:
   - The live camera feed is displayed in the centre of the screen. Here, you can see what the drone sees in real-time.
   - You can access camera settings by tapping the gear icon, where you can adjust resolution, frame rate, and other settings.

3. **Flight Modes**:
   - On the left side of the screen, you can toggle between different flight modes (e.g., Normal, Sport, and CineSmooth). Each mode offers varying levels of responsiveness and speed, tailored for different flying styles.

4. **Telemetry Data**:
   - The telemetry data is displayed on the screen, showing important information such as altitude, distance from the home point, flight time, and speed.
   - You can customize the telemetry data displayed by tapping on the settings icon.

5. **Settings Menu**:
   - The settings menu allows you to adjust various drone settings, including safety features, control sensitivity, and customizable button assignments.

6. **Accessing Tutorials and Help**:
   - The app includes tutorials and help resources accessible from the home screen, providing guidance on different flight features and settings.

Understanding Flight Telemetry

Flight telemetry provides real-time data about your drone's status and performance, which is critical for safe and efficient flying. Here's what you need to know:

1. **Altitude**:
   - Displays how high the drone is flying. Keep an eye on this to avoid flying too high in restricted airspace.

2. **Distance from Home Point**:
   - Indicates how far the drone is from its takeoff point. This is crucial for ensuring a safe return, especially if the battery runs low.
3. **Battery Level**:
   - Shows the current battery percentage. Make sure to monitor this to prevent unexpected landings.
4. **GPS Signal Strength**:
   - Provides information on the number of satellites connected. A higher satellite count (ideally above 7) ensures better positioning and stability.
5. **Flight Time**:
   - Tracks how long the drone has been flying. This helps you manage battery life and plan your flights accordingly.
6. **Speed**:
   - Displays the current speed of the drone, helping you understand how quickly it's moving in the air.

Understanding the DJI Fly app and flight telemetry, will enhance your piloting skills and ensure a safer, more enjoyable flying experience.

6.

Flight Modes and Intelligent Features

The DJI Air 3S offers several flight modes and intelligent features to help you capture cinematic footage and enjoy a customized flying experience. Here's an overview of the different modes, how to switch between them, and a guide to using pre-programmed shots through **QuickShots**.

Normal, Sport, and Cine Modes

The DJI Air 3S comes with three main flight modes, each offering a different balance between speed, agility, and smoothness.

1. **Normal Mode**:
   - **Best for**: Everyday flying and general use.
   - **Performance**: In this mode, the drone operates at moderate speeds, and obstacle sensors are enabled to help you avoid collisions.
   - It provides a stable flying experience, making it perfect for beginners or casual flights where safety is key.

2. **Sport Mode**:
   - **Best for**: High-speed flights.
   - **Performance**: The drone reaches its maximum speed and becomes much more responsive to the controls. Obstacle avoidance is **disabled** in this mode, so it's important to fly with caution.
   - Ideal for capturing fast-moving subjects, racing, or flying in open areas where obstacles aren't a concern.

3. **Cine Mode (CineSmooth):**
   - **Best for:** Capturing cinematic footage.
   - **Performance:** The drone's movements are slower and more deliberate, giving you smoother, more controlled shots. It reduces speed and increases control sensitivity for precision flying.
   - Perfect for slow, smooth shots when filming landscapes or when precision is required.

Differences Between Modes
- **Speed:**
  - Sport Mode is the fastest, while Cine Mode is the slowest.
- **Obstacle Avoidance:**
  - Enabled in Normal and Cine modes, disabled in Sport mode.
- **Control Sensitivity:**
  - Sport Mode offers the most responsive control, while Cine Mode provides a slower, more deliberate feel.

How to Switch Modes
Switching between modes is simple and can be done directly through the remote controller or the DJI Fly app:
1. **Using the Remote Controller:**
   - There is a dedicated **Mode switch** on the remote that allows you to toggle between **Normal**, **Sport**, and **Cine** modes easily.

2. **Using the DJI Fly App**:
   - You can also switch modes via the **flight mode toggle** on the DJI Fly app's interface. It's located on the left side of the screen and will show the current mode.

How to Use QuickShots Pre-Programmed Shots

QuickShots are pre-programmed flight patterns that allow the drone to capture dynamic footage automatically. You can focus on your subject while the DJI Air 3S performs the movements. Here are the most popular QuickShots available:

1. **Dronie**:
   - The drone flies backwards and upward while keeping the subject in the frame. Perfect for pulling away to reveal the landscape or environment.
   - **How to use**: Select the **Dronie** option in the DJI Fly app, set the subject, and tap **Start**.

2. **Circle**:
   - The drone flies in a circular path around the subject while keeping the camera pointed at it. Great for capturing a 360-degree view.
   - **How to use**: Choose **Circle** in the app, define the subject, and start the QuickShot.

3. **Rocket**:
   - The drone flies straight up while the camera tilts downward to focus on the subject. It's perfect for a dramatic overhead reveal shot.
   - **How to use**: Select **Rocket**, lock onto the subject and start the shot.

4. **Boomerang**:
   - The drone flies an oval path around the subject, ascending as it moves outward and then descending as it comes back.
   - **How to use**: Tap **Boomerang** in the QuickShots menu, choose the subject, and tap **Start**.
5. **Helix**:
   - The drone spirals up and away from the subject, creating a dynamic and cinematic pull-back shot.
   - **How to use**: Pick **Helix**, set the distance, and start the shot. The drone will automatically perform the complex movement.

Using QuickShots: Step-by-Step

1. **Launch the DJI Fly App**:
   - Connect your drone, power it on, and open the DJI Fly app.
2. **Navigate to QuickShots**:
   - Tap on the QuickShots icon on the main interface to see the available pre-programmed shots.
3. **Select Your QuickShot**:
   - Choose from **Dronie, Circle, Rocket, Boomerang, Helix**, or other QuickShot options.
4. **Define Your Subject**:
   - Use the app to draw a box around the subject you want the drone to track.
5. **Start the Shot**:

- Once your subject is set, tap **Start** and watch as the DJI Air 3S performs the manoeuvre automatically while keeping your subject in focus.

These modes and QuickShot features give you a ton of creative flexibility when capturing footage. Experiment with each mode to find the one that works best for your flying style or the shot you're looking to capture!

How to Use FocusTrack Features

The **FocusTrack** suite in the DJI Air 3S offers three intelligent flight features that make it easier to capture complex shots by automatically keeping the subject in frame. These include **ActiveTrack**, **Spotlight**, and **Point of Interest (POI)**.

ActiveTrack

- **What it does**: ActiveTrack allows the drone to follow a moving subject while keeping it centred in the frame. It works even if the subject moves in different directions or speeds.

- **How to use**: Select the subject in the DJI Fly app by drawing a box around it. The drone will begin tracking the subject automatically, adjusting its position to stay in sync with the movement.

Spotlight

- **What it does**: In Spotlight mode, the drone locks the camera on the subject but gives you full control over its flight. You can manually move the drone while the camera stays focused on the subject, giving you more creative freedom.

- **How to use**: Choose **Spotlight** from the FocusTrack menu and select your subject. While you control the drone's flight path, the camera will automatically keep the subject in the frame.

Point of Interest (POI)

- **What it does**: POI allows the drone to fly in a circular pattern around a designated subject, keeping the camera focused on it. This is great for capturing 360-degree views of a static subject.
- **How to use**: Select POI in the DJI Fly app, choose the object you want to circle, and set the desired distance and speed. The drone will automatically perform the orbit.

How to Record with MasterShots

MasterShots is an intelligent shooting mode that automates the process of capturing dynamic, cinematic footage. The drone performs a series of pre-programmed manoeuvres while the camera focuses on your subject, creating a professional-looking video in minutes.

- **How to use MasterShots**:
    1. **Launch the DJI Fly App** and navigate to the camera view.
    2. Tap the **MasterShots** icon and select your subject by drawing a box around it.
    3. The app will then automatically plan a sequence of shots, including **Dronie, Rocket, Circle, Helix**, and more.
    4. Once the sequence is complete, you can use the app to edit and export the video with transitions and effects.

MasterShots is designed for quick and easy cinematic footage, perfect for creating dynamic content without manually planning complex manoeuvres.

Using Waypoints for Custom Flight Paths

Waypoints allow you to pre-program a flight path for the drone, which it will follow autonomously. This feature is ideal for mapping out precise routes and capturing specific shots at multiple angles, especially useful in surveying, real estate, and time-lapse photography.

- **How to use Waypoints**:
    1. Open the **DJI Fly App** and select the **Waypoints** mode.
    2. Fly the drone manually to your desired locations and mark each waypoint in the app.
    3. After setting the waypoints, you can adjust the altitude, speed, and direction at each point.
    4. Start the mission, and the drone will fly through each waypoint autonomously, allowing you to focus on operating the camera or reviewing the footage.

Waypoints add a new level of precision to your shots and are great for repeating the same flight path for consistency in projects like time-lapses or progress tracking.

With these intelligent features, the DJI Air 3S offers unparalleled control and flexibility that allows you to capture stunning footage effortlessly.

7.

Advanced Flying Techniques

To take full advantage of the DJI Air 3S's capabilities, it's essential to understand its **Obstacle Avoidance System** and how to adjust the flight settings to suit your flying style. Here's a breakdown of these advanced techniques to help you fly more confidently and get smoother shots.

Obstacle Avoidance System

The DJI Air 3S is equipped with an advanced obstacle sensing and avoidance system to help prevent collisions during flight. Here's how it works and how to use it effectively:

How It Works

- The drone uses a combination of forward, backwards, downward, and sideward sensors to detect obstacles in its flight path.
- When an obstacle is detected, the drone can either stop and hover or, if enabled, automatically reroute itself to avoid the object.
- In **ActiveTrack** and **QuickShots** modes, obstacle avoidance plays a crucial role in ensuring the drone follows the subject safely while avoiding obstacles in its path.

How to Use It Effectively

- **Enable Obstacle Avoidance**: In the DJI Fly app, make sure obstacle avoidance is enabled. This can usually be found in the **Safety** settings tab.
- **Flying in Tight Spaces**: In narrow or cluttered environments, it's helpful to fly in **CineSmooth** mode, as the reduced speed

allows the sensors more time to detect obstacles and the drone to react accordingly.

- **Obstacle Avoidance Settings**:
    - You can customize how the drone reacts to obstacles—either it will stop and hover or actively reroute itself. This setting can be found under **Safety** in the app.

Tips for Effective Use:

- **Always keep an eye on the environment**: Even with obstacle avoidance, certain objects (like thin branches or wires) may not be detected. Always visually monitor the flight.
- **Update Firmware Regularly**: DJI often updates their obstacle avoidance algorithms, so keeping your firmware updated ensures the best possible performance.

Adjusting Flight Sensitivity and Settings

To fine-tune your flying experience, DJI allows you to adjust the drone's flight sensitivity, speed, and control responsiveness. These settings can significantly affect how the drone handles in different environments or shooting situations.

Customizing Flight Controls

You can personalize the flight controls to match your experience level or preference:

1. **Flight Control Modes**: DJI drones come with preset control modes, but you can switch between them or even create custom configurations:
    - **Mode 2** (default): Left stick for altitude and rotation, right stick for forward/backward and sideways movements.

- You can adjust the control sensitivity under **Control Settings** in the app, allowing for smoother or sharper responses to joystick input.

2. **Yaw and Gimbal Speed**:
   - **Yaw Sensitivity** adjusts how fast the drone turns. For cinematic shots, slower yaw speeds will give you smoother pans.
   - **Gimbal Speed** controls how fast the camera tilts. Lower speeds provide smoother camera tilts, which is useful for professional-looking footage.

Adjusting Speed and Responsiveness

1. **Max Speed Settings**: You can set the maximum speed for each flight mode (Normal, Sport, and CineSmooth). For example:
   - In **Sport Mode**, you might want the highest speed for fast flights.
   - In **CineSmooth Mode**, slower speeds help you create smoother, more cinematic shots.

2. **Expo Settings**: These settings adjust how responsive the drone is to the movement of the joysticks:
   - **High Expo**: Makes the drone react quickly to slight stick movements.
   - **Low Expo**: Makes the drone react more slowly and smoothly to stick inputs—ideal for precise movements during filming.

Flight Settings Walkthrough:

1. Open the **DJI Fly App** and go to **Control Settings**.
2. From here, you can adjust:

- **Stick Sensitivity**: Customize how quickly the drone reacts to stick movements.
- **Braking Sensitivity**: Adjust how quickly the drone comes to a stop after you release the controls.
- **Yaw and Pitch Sensitivity**: Fine-tune the responsiveness of the drone's rotational movements.

Adjust these settings to find the right balance between control precision and responsiveness for your flying style. Mastering the **Obstacle Avoidance System** and customizing the flight controls are key to improving your flying techniques with the DJI Air 3S. By adjusting and controlling these settings, you can tailor the drone's performance to capture the best shots, whether you're flying fast or aiming for smooth, cinematic footage.

How to Fly in No-GPS Environments

Flying your DJI Air 3S drone in environments without GPS, such as indoors or in areas with poor satellite reception, can be tricky, but it's manageable with the right preparation. Here's how you can effectively navigate these situations:

Switching to ATTI (Attitude) Mode

When GPS is unavailable, the drone switches to **ATTI Mode**. In this mode, the drone stabilizes its altitude but doesn't hold its position automatically, meaning it can drift with wind or momentum. Here's what to consider:

- **Flight Control**: You'll need to manually control the drone's position using the joysticks, adjusting for any drift.
- **Visual Positioning System (VPS)**: The DJI Air 3S has downward-facing sensors to help with altitude control and slight position stabilization, which works well for indoor flights.

- **Use Tripod Mode**: For indoor or close-quarters flying, switching to **Tripod Mode** (or CineSmooth) can help slow down the drone's movements and provide more precision.

Tips for Flying Without GPS:

- **Practice in an open space first** to get used to ATTI Mode, as you'll need to control all movements manually.
- **Keep the altitude low** when flying indoors or in areas without GPS to avoid sudden drifts or crashes.
- **Avoid windy conditions**, as the drone will be more prone to drift in ATTI Mode.
- **Monitor the drone's movements carefully** and be prepared to adjust the controls quickly to compensate for any unexpected shifts.

How to Perform Advanced Maneuvers

Mastering advanced manoeuvres allows you to capture more dynamic footage and enhances your control over the drone. Here are a few advanced flying techniques you can practice:

Orbiting a Subject Manually

This manoeuvre is useful for creating cinematic 360-degree shots around a subject without relying on automated modes like POI (Point of Interest).

1. **Maintain Constant Distance**: Fly sideways while using the yaw control (left stick) to rotate the drone continuously around the subject.
2. **Focus on the Subject**: Keep the camera centred on the subject as you orbit to ensure smooth footage.

Manual Tracking

Instead of relying on **ActiveTrack**, you can manually track a moving subject:

1. **Fly Forward or Sideways** while adjusting yaw to keep the subject centred.

2. **Practice Smooth Movements**: Avoid jerky stick inputs. Gradually adjust the controls for smooth, professional-looking tracking shots.

Precision Landings

Landing the drone manually in a tight spot or on a small platform (like a drone pad) is an essential skill for advanced pilots:

1. **Slow Descent**: Reduce the descent speed as you approach the landing zone to maintain control.

2. **Spot Control**: Make micro-adjustments to the left and right sticks to ensure you're directly over your intended landing spot.

Backwards Flying with Object Avoidance

Flying backwards is a great way to reveal large landscapes or subjects in your shots:

1. **Use Object Avoidance Sensors** to ensure you don't back into any obstacles.

2. **Fly at a Consistent Speed**: For cinematic shots, use **CineSmooth** mode or adjust the gimbal pitch smoothly as the drone flies backwards to keep the subject in the frame.

By mastering these advanced manoeuvres and preparing for no-GPS environments, you'll be ready to handle any flight situation and capture impressive footage.

8.

Aerial Photography and Videography

When using the DJI Air 3S for aerial photography and videography, understanding the camera settings and modes is key to capturing high-quality images and footage. The Air 3S comes with advanced camera specs that offer flexibility and creative control, from **Auto** mode for beginners to **Pro** settings for more experienced users.

Camera, Specs and Settings

- **Camera Sensor**: The DJI Air 3S is equipped with a **1-inch CMOS sensor**, which captures stunning detail and performs well in various lighting conditions.

- **Video Resolution**: It supports up to **5.4K at 30 fps** and **4K at 60 fps**, ensuring crisp and smooth footage, even during fast movements.

- **Photo Resolution**: You can capture 20 MP still images, perfect for high-resolution landscape shots.

- **Dynamic Range**: With a high dynamic range, the camera captures greater detail in both shadows and highlights, making it suitable for challenging lighting conditions.

- **Zoom Capability**: The camera offers up to **4x digital zoom**, which allows for close-up shots without physically moving the drone closer to the subject.

Camera Modes

- **Auto Mode**: In **Auto Mode**, the camera automatically adjusts settings like ISO, shutter speed, and white balance based on the scene. This mode is perfect for beginners or those looking to capture great footage quickly without having to adjust settings manually.

- **Pro Mode**: **Pro Mode** (or manual mode) gives you full control over camera settings, allowing you to fine-tune ISO, shutter speed, and white balance to your preference. This mode is ideal for advanced users who want more control over the exposure and image quality.

- **HDR Mode**: The DJI Air 3S also offers an **HDR** mode, which captures multiple exposures and combines them into one image for better detail in both bright and dark areas.

- **Panorama Mode**: For landscape shots, **Panorama Mode** can stitch together multiple images, providing an ultra-wide perspective.

Adjusting ISO, Shutter Speed, and White Balance

ISO Settings:

- **What it does**: ISO controls the camera's sensitivity to light. A lower ISO (e.g., 100) is best for bright daylight, while a higher ISO (e.g., 800 or 1600) is used in low-light conditions.

- **How to adjust**: In **Pro Mode**, you can manually adjust ISO to control the brightness of your shot. Keep the ISO as low as possible to reduce noise and maintain image quality.

Shutter Speed:

- **What it does**: Shutter speed determines how long the camera's sensor is exposed to light. A fast shutter speed (e.g., 1/1000 sec) is ideal for freezing motion, while a slower shutter speed (e.g., 1/30 sec) can introduce motion blur, which is sometimes used creatively in video.

- **How to adjust**: In **Pro Mode**, adjust the shutter speed based on the amount of light and the effect you want to achieve. For smooth video, follow the **180-degree rule**: set your shutter speed to roughly **double** your frame rate (e.g., for 30 fps video, use a 1/60 sec shutter speed).

White Balance:

- **What it does**: White balance controls the colour temperature of your footage, ensuring that whites appear white, and colours look natural.

- **Auto White Balance (AWB)**: In **Auto Mode**, the drone automatically adjusts the white balance, which works well in most conditions.

- **Manual White Balance**: In **Pro Mode**, you can set the white balance manually depending on the lighting conditions:
    - **Daylight** (~5500K) for sunny conditions.
    - **Tungsten** (~3200K) for indoor lighting.
    - **Cloudy** (~6500K) for overcast skies.

Adjusting these settings in **Pro Mode** gives you maximum creative control over your shots, ensuring that you can achieve the exact look and feel you're aiming for in your aerial photography and videography.

Capturing High-Quality Photos

The DJI Air 3S offers advanced features for capturing stunning aerial photos. Whether you're interested in panoramas, time-lapses, or hyper lapses, the drone has versatile modes to help you capture high-quality images in a variety of settings.

Shooting Panoramas

Panorama mode stitches together multiple images to create a wide, expansive shot, ideal for landscapes.

1. **Select Panorama Mode**: Open the **DJI Fly App**, go to the camera settings, and choose **Panorama**.
2. **Choose the Type of Panorama**:
    - **180° Panorama**: Captures a wide-angle view in a single direction.
    - **360° Panorama**: Automatically takes multiple photos to create a full spherical image.
    - **Wide-Angle**: Captures multiple images and stitches them into one wide-angle shot.
3. **Take the Shot**: The drone will automatically capture and process the images into one seamless panorama.

Tips:

- Use a higher resolution for more detailed panoramas.
- Ensure your drone is at a stable altitude to avoid any distortions in the stitched image.

Shooting Time-Lapses and hyper lapses

Time-lapse and hyper-lapse modes let you condense long periods into short, dynamic video sequences.

1. **Time-Lapse**:
    - **How to Set It Up**: Select **Time-Lapse Mode** in the app. Set the interval (e.g., 2 seconds) and duration of the time-lapse.
    - **Ideal Uses**: Great for capturing slow-moving scenes like sunsets or clouds drifting over landscapes.
2. **Hyperlapse**:

- **How It Works**: Unlike time-lapse, **Hyperlapse** involves moving the drone while recording. The drone automatically captures a series of images at set intervals and combines them into a smooth video.

- **Types of Hyperlapses**:

Free Mode: Fly manually while the drone captures images.

Circle Mode: The drone automatically flies in a circle around a subject.

Course Lock Mode: The drone flies along a fixed path, perfect for dramatic landscape shots.

Waypoint Mode: Set specific GPS waypoints, and the drone will fly between them while capturing images.

Tips:

- Choose a lower interval (e.g., 1-2 seconds) for smoother results.
- For hyper lapses, use ND filters to balance exposure over time, especially in changing light conditions.

Recording Professional-Quality Videos

To create professional-grade videos, understanding the camera's resolution, frame rate, and colour profile settings is key. The DJI Air 3S offers flexible settings that let you tailor your footage based on your shooting needs.

Resolution and Frame Rate

- **Resolution Options**: The Air 3S supports up to **5.4K resolution** at **30 fps**, which is ideal for capturing fine details in landscapes or wide shots.

- **Frame Rates**: For smoother footage, use:
    - **24 fps** for a cinematic look.
    - **30 fps** for standard videos.
    - **60 fps** for fluid motion or slow-motion playback when recording at **4K** resolution.

Tips:

- **5.4K at 30 fps** offers high detail and quality, but if you need smoother slow motion, switch to **4K at 60 fps**.
- **1080p at 120 fps** is ideal for super-slow-motion shots.

Colour Profile Settings

- **Normal Mode**: Suitable for casual use with well-balanced colour and contrast.
- **D-Cinelike**: This is a **flat colour profile** that retains a more dynamic range, which is ideal for professional editing and colour grading in post-production.

Tips:

- Use **D-Cinelike** when planning to colour grade in post-processing for greater flexibility.
- Shoot in **Normal Mode** if you prefer to minimize editing and need a quicker turnaround.

Using Gimbal Settings for Smooth Shots

The **gimbal** on the DJI Air 3S is key to capturing smooth, stable footage, even during fast manoeuvres. Adjusting the gimbal settings ensures your shots look polished and professional.

Gimbal Mode Options

1. **Follow Mode**: The camera smoothly follows the drone's movements, ideal for most types of footage.

2. **FPV Mode**: The camera tilts with the drone's movements, giving a more immersive, first-person view, perfect for action shots or dynamic flying.

3. **Tilt-Lock Mode**: Locks the camera's tilt angle, so it stays level even if the drone is tilting or flying at an angle.

Adjusting Gimbal Speed

1. **Gimbal Pitch Speed**: You can adjust how fast the gimbal moves up and down using the **DJI Fly App**.

    - **Lower Pitch Speed**: Use slower speeds for smoother, cinematic tilts.

    - **Higher Pitch Speed**: Set to faster speeds for action-oriented shots where quick gimbal movements are needed.

2. **Gimbal Pitch Smoothness**: Adjust how smooth or abrupt the gimbal movements are.

    - A higher smoothness value will slow down and smooth out the transition between gimbal positions.

Tips:

- For professional-quality footage, keep gimbal movements slow and smooth, especially when panning or tilting the camera.

- Regularly calibrate the gimbal for optimal stability, especially after travelling with the drone.

When you master these techniques for **capturing high-quality photos**, **recording professional-grade videos**, and **using gimbal settings**, you can take full advantage of the DJI Air 3S's powerful camera features for stunning aerial shots.

9.

Post-Flight Procedures

After flying the DJI Air 3S, following a proper post-flight process ensures that both the drone and your data are safe and secure. This section walks you through **safe landing techniques**, how to **power off the drone and controller**, and **how to transfer your media** for editing or sharing.

Safe Landing Techniques

Landing your drone safely is a crucial part of flight operation. Here's how you can do it smoothly:

1. **Manual Landing**:
    - **Slow Descent**: Use the left joystick to gently lower the drone by pushing it down slowly, keeping an eye on the ground.
    - **Flat Surface**: Ensure you're landing on a flat and stable surface free from obstacles.
    - **Final Descent**: As the drone approaches the ground, continue to reduce the speed of descent until it touches down softly.

2. **Auto-Landing**:
    - The DJI Air 3S offers an **auto-landing** feature. In the **DJI Fly App**, tap the **Auto-Land** button, and the drone will descend to the ground automatically.
    - This is especially useful when you're flying in **Beginner Mode** or need a more hands-off approach.

Tips:

- Always check your landing area for obstacles or uneven surfaces.
- Avoid landing on gravel or sand to prevent particles from getting into the motors.

Powering Off the Drone and Remote Controller

1. **Powering Off the Drone**:
    - **Press** the power button on the battery once to check the battery level.
    - **Press and hold** the button again until the drone powers down completely.
2. **Powering Off the Remote Controller**:
    - Like the drone, **press the power button** on the controller once, then **press and hold** until it turns off.
    - Make sure the controller has no active connections before powering it down.

Reviewing and Transferring Media

Once your flight is complete, you'll want to review and transfer your photos and videos. The DJI Air 3S allows for quick media access through the **DJI Fly App**, and transferring files to your computer or cloud storage is a straightforward process.

Accessing Photos and Videos on the DJI Fly App:

1. **Open the App**: After landing and powering down, keep the drone connected to the remote and app.
2. **Go to the Album**: In the app, tap the **Album** icon to view the media captured during your flight.

3. **Quick Review**: You can immediately preview your photos and videos from the app without transferring them.

Transferring Files to Your Computer:

1. **Remove the MicroSD Card**: The quickest way to transfer large files is to remove the **microSD card** from the drone and use a card reader to transfer them to your computer.

2. **Via USB Cable**:

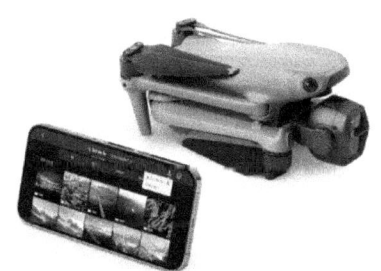

Off-State QuickTransfer

You can now send files from your Air 3S to a smartphone even when the drone is powered off. [8] Transfers to a computer can also be done with the drone powered off—simply connect Air 3S via a compatible USB cable.

- Connect the drone directly to your computer using a **USB-C cable**.
- Turn the drone on, and your computer should recognize it as a storage device, allowing you to drag and drop files.

Transferring Files to Cloud Storage:

1. **Using DJI Fly App**:

- If you prefer cloud storage, the DJI Fly App has integration with some cloud services. Select your media and upload it directly to your **preferred cloud service** (Google Drive, Dropbox, etc.).

2. **DJI QuickTransfer**:

    - The **QuickTransfer** feature allows you to wirelessly transfer high-resolution files from the drone to your phone, from where you can upload them to the cloud.

    - This is useful if you want to review and edit footage on the go.

Tips:

- Keep your microSD cards organized to avoid confusion, especially after multiple flights.
- Use a high-speed card reader for faster transfer times, especially with large 4K or 5.4K videos.

These post-flight procedures can maintain the longevity of your DJI Air 3S while ensuring you have quick access to your media for review and editing.

10.

Drone Maintenance

Proper maintenance is key to keeping your drone in peak condition for every flight. Learn how to clean your drone, store it correctly, maintain the batteries, and ensure that your firmware and software are always up-to-date.

Cleaning the Drone and Camera Lens

Keeping your drone and camera lens clean is essential for optimal performance and image quality.

1. **Cleaning the Drone**:
   - **Wipe the Exterior**: Use a soft, microfiber cloth to wipe down the drone's body and propellers to remove dust, dirt, and fingerprints. For harder-to-reach areas, like vents or motor gaps, use compressed air to gently blow away debris.
   - **Check for Debris**: After flights in dusty or grassy areas, inspect the motors and propellers for small particles that could affect flight performance.

2. **Cleaning the Camera Lens**:
   - **Use Lens Cleaner**: Clean the lens with a camera-specific lens cleaner or alcohol wipe. Always use a soft lens cloth to avoid scratches.
   - **Avoid Direct Contact**: Minimize touching the lens with your fingers to prevent oil or smudges that could affect the quality of your footage.

Tips:

- Never use water directly on the drone or lens, as it could damage the electronics.
- Perform regular cleanings after each flight to prevent build-up, especially if flying in sandy or wet environments.

Storing the Drone and Accessories

Proper storage of your drone and its accessories can help prolong their lifespan and ensure they're always ready for your next flight.

1. **Store in a Cool, Dry Place**: Keep your drone in a temperature-controlled environment away from direct sunlight, extreme cold, or high humidity.
2. **Use a Hard Case**: For added protection, store the drone and accessories in a hard, padded case. This prevents damage from impacts during transport.
3. **Propeller Storage**: Remove or fold the propellers (if foldable) before storing to avoid damage or warping.
4. **Keep Accessories Together**: Organize accessories like batteries, chargers, and extra propellers in separate compartments to avoid tangling or damage.

Tips:

- Avoid leaving the drone in a car on hot or cold days as temperature extremes can damage the internal components and battery.

Battery Maintenance and Storage Tips

Maintaining your DJI Air 3S batteries properly will extend their life and ensure consistent power during flights.

1. **Battery Storage**:

- **Optimal Charge for Storage**: Store your batteries at around 50% charge if you won't be using the drone for an extended period (a week or more). Fully charged or completely depleted batteries can degrade over time.

- **Temperature Considerations**: Store the batteries in a cool, dry environment (around 22°C or 72°F). Avoid storing them in direct sunlight or cold environments.

2. **Charging Tips**:

   - **Avoid Overcharging**: Once the battery reaches 100%, unplug it from the charger to avoid overcharging, which can reduce its lifespan.

   - **Charge Before Flight**: Always charge your batteries fully before each flight, but don't leave them fully charged for more than a few days without use.

3. **Battery Health Check**:

   - **Use DJI Fly App**: Regularly check the battery health in the DJI Fly App to ensure no cells are damaged. If any abnormalities are detected, it's best to replace the battery.

Tips:

- Never charge the battery immediately after a flight when it's still hot. Allow it to cool down first.
- Avoid draining the battery completely before recharging, as this can shorten its lifespan.

Updating Firmware and Software Regularly

DJI frequently releases updates for performance enhancements and compatibility with the latest devices.

1. **How to Update Firmware**:

- **Via the DJI Fly App**: The DJI Fly App will prompt you when a new firmware update is available for your drone or controller. Ensure your drone and controller are fully charged before starting the update process.
- **Steps**:
    1. Connect your drone to the DJI Fly App.
    2. If an update is available, follow the on-screen instructions to download and install it.
    3. The drone will automatically restart once the update is complete.

2. **Importance of Software Updates**:
    - **DJI Fly App Updates**: Keep the DJI Fly App updated to ensure compatibility with your drone's firmware and access to the latest features.
    - **Fix Bugs and Enhance Performance**: Firmware updates often include fixes for any issues discovered after the drone's release, so updating ensures your drone remains stable during flights.

Troubleshooting Common Issues

Even with a high-quality drone like the DJI Air 3S, occasional issues can arise. Some common problems, like connection issues and calibration errors, can be resolved.

How to Handle Connection Problems

1. Drone Not Connecting to the Remote Controller If your DJI Air 3S is having trouble connecting to the remote controller, try these steps:

- **Ensure Both Devices Are Powered On**: Double-check that both the drone and the remote controller are turned on.
- **Re-Pair the Devices**:
    1. Turn on the drone and controller.
    2. Press and hold the **pairing button** on the drone until you hear a beep.
    3. Press the **pairing button** on the remote controller to sync.
    4. The devices should now reconnect.
- **Check the USB Cable**: If you're connecting through a cable, make sure the USB cable isn't damaged and is properly plugged into both the controller and your mobile device.

2. Drone Not Connecting to the DJI Fly App

- **Update Firmware**: Ensure both the drone and the DJI Fly App are updated to the latest version. Sometimes connection issues arise from incompatible versions.
- **Restart Both Devices**: Power off both the drone and your mobile device, then turn them back on to refresh the connection.
- **Check Phone Settings**: Make sure your phone's **Wi-Fi** and **Bluetooth** are enabled, as they're essential for communication between your device and the drone.

Solving Calibration Errors

1. Compass Calibration Errors Compass calibration is crucial for stable flight and accurate GPS readings. If you're receiving a compass calibration error:

- **Recalibrate the Compass**:

1. Open the **DJI Fly App** and go to the settings menu.
2. Navigate to **Compass Calibration** and follow the on-screen instructions.
3. Rotate the drone as directed by the app until the calibration is complete.

- **Avoid Magnetic Interference**: Calibration should be done away from large metal objects, vehicles, or electronics that could interfere with the compass.

2. IMU Calibration Errors The Inertial Measurement Unit (IMU) measures your drone's orientation, and calibration errors can lead to unstable flight.

- **How to Calibrate the IMU**:
    1. In the **DJI Fly App**, go to the settings menu.
    2. Navigate to **IMU Calibration** and follow the on-screen steps.
    3. Place the drone on a flat, stable surface and allow it to complete the calibration process.
- **Tips**: Make sure the drone remains completely still during calibration to avoid errors.

11.

Legal Considerations and No-Fly Zones

Operating a drone like the DJI Air 3S involves more than just technical know-how; you also need to be aware of legal and regulatory requirements. Below are key legal aspects, including FAA registration, local drone laws, no-fly zones, and how to apply for airspace authorization.

Understanding Local Drone Laws and Regulations

Before you take your DJI Air 3S for a flight, it's important to familiarize yourself with the local laws and regulations regarding drone usage. Rules vary depending on the country or region, but common regulations include:

- **Altitude Restrictions**: Most countries have limits on how high you can fly your drone (typically around 400 feet in the U.S.).
- **Line of Sight**: You are required to maintain visual contact with your drone at all times during the flight.
- **Restricted Areas**: You cannot fly in certain locations like airports, military bases, and government facilities without special permission.

To ensure you're compliant, always check the specific regulations in your country before flying.

Tips:

- In the **U.S.**, the **Federal Aviation Administration (FAA)** sets the rules, while in the **UK**, it's the **Civil Aviation Authority (CAA)**. Always check the official website of your country's aviation authority for the latest updates.

FAA Registration and Certifications (for U.S. Users)

As of the time of writing this- if you're flying in the U.S., the **FAA** requires all drones over **0.55 lbs (250g)**, including the DJI Air 3S, to be registered.

1. **How to Register**:
    - Go to the **FAA DroneZone** website (https://faadronezone.faa.gov).
    - Create an account or log in if you already have one.
    - Register your drone by entering its serial number and pay the registration fee (usually $5).
    - You will receive a registration number that must be affixed to your drone.

2. **Part 107 Certification**:
    - If you plan to use your drone for commercial purposes (e.g., real estate photography, and inspections), you will need to pass the FAA's **Part 107 Certification** exam.
    - This certification ensures that you understand the rules of flying drones commercially and includes topics like airspace classifications, weather patterns, and emergency procedures.

Tip:
- If you're flying strictly for recreational purposes, you do not need the Part 107 Certification, but you still need to follow safety rules set by the FAA.

No-Fly Zones and How to Identify Them

Flying in no-fly zones can result in hefty fines or drone confiscation. No-fly zones are areas where drones are restricted or prohibited entirely, often for safety or security reasons.

1. **How to Identify No-Fly Zones**:
   - **DJI FlySafe Map**: DJI offers a **FlySafe** map that shows restricted areas. You can access this feature directly in the **DJI Fly App** or online at the **FlySafe** website (https://www.dji.com/flysafe).
   - **B4UFLY App**: The **FAA's B4UFLY app** is another useful tool for checking airspace restrictions in the U.S. It shows nearby airports, controlled airspace, and other restricted areas.
   - **Local Authorities**: Always check with your local government or aviation authority, as additional restrictions may apply in certain areas (e.g., parks, and wildlife reserves).

Examples of No-Fly Zones:
- Airports and their surrounding areas
- National parks
- Military installations
- Special events like concerts or sports games (TFRs: Temporary Flight Restrictions)

How to Apply for Airspace Authorization

If you need to fly your DJI Air 3S in controlled airspace or a restricted area, you'll need to apply for authorization.

1. **Applying for Airspace Authorization**:

- **LAANC (Low Altitude Authorization and Notification Capability)**: In the U.S., you can use the **LAANC system** to request near-real-time authorization to fly in controlled airspace.
- **FAA DroneZone**: For more complex flights, or areas not covered by LAANC, you may need to submit an airspace authorization request through the FAA's **DroneZone** portal.
- **DJI FlySafe Unlock**: In some cases, DJI FlySafe will allow you to unlock restricted zones for approved flights. Visit the **FlySafe Unlocking System** on the DJI website to apply for temporary access.

2. **What to Include in Your Request**:
    - Details of your flight (location, time, altitude)
    - Reason for requesting access
    - Your drone's registration number and operator certification (if required)

Tip:
- **Apply Early**: Airspace authorizations can take some time, so make sure to apply well in advance of your planned flight.

By understanding local drone laws, registering with the appropriate authorities, and respecting no-fly zones, you'll be flying your DJI Air 3S safely and legally every time.

12.

Troubleshooting General Issues and Solutions

1. **Drone Won't Connect to the Remote Controller**

    - **Solution**: Ensure both the drone and remote controller are powered on. Try re-pairing them by pressing the pairing button on both devices. If problems persist, check your mobile device's connection settings (Bluetooth and Wi-Fi).

2. **Loss of GPS Signal**

    - **Solution**: Ensure you're in an open area away from tall buildings or heavy foliage that might obstruct the GPS signal. Restart the drone and give it a moment to recalibrate. If GPS issues continue, consider recalibrating the compass via the DJI Fly app.

3. **Battery Not Charging**

    - **Solution**: Inspect the battery and charger for any visible damage. Use a different charging cable or power outlet to rule out issues. If the battery still won't charge, it may need to be replaced.

4. **Camera Not Responding**

    - **Solution**: Restart the drone. Ensure the camera lens is clean and free from obstructions. If the problem continues, check for firmware updates in the DJI Fly app.

5. **Drone Crashes or Erratic Flight Behavior**

    - **Solution**: Check for any physical damage to the drone or propellers. Ensure that the drone's firmware is up to date. Conduct a compass and IMU calibration before the next flight.

How to Reset the Drone

If you encounter persistent issues that troubleshooting can't resolve, resetting the DJI Air 3S to factory settings might help. Here's how:

1. **Using the DJI Fly App**:

    - Open the **DJI Fly App**.

    - Connect your drone and navigate to the **Settings** menu.

    - Find the option for **Reset Settings** or **Factory Reset**.

    - Follow the prompts to complete the reset process.

2. **Hard Reset**:

    - Power off the drone.

    - Press and hold the power button for about 9 seconds until the indicators flash to reset the drone.

    - Release the power button and wait for the drone to reboot.

Note: Resetting your drone will erase all custom settings and configurations, so proceed with caution.

Contacting DJI Support

If issues persist after troubleshooting and resetting, it's time to reach out to DJI support. Here's how:

1. **DJI Support Website**:

- Visit the DJI Support page for comprehensive resources, including FAQs, guides, and the option to submit a support ticket.

2. **Live Chat and Phone Support**:
    - Use the live chat feature on the DJI website for immediate assistance, or call DJI support directly for complex issues that require in-depth troubleshooting.

3. **DJI Forum and Community**:
    - Consider visiting the DJI Forum where you can connect with other DJI users for tips and shared experiences.

www.ingramcontent.com/pod-product-compliance
Lightning Source LLC
Chambersburg PA
CBHW070401230526
45471CB00006B/2656